WILDCAT ON THE SHORELINE

WILDCAT ON THE SHORELINE

Poems by

Lee A. Jacobus

Antrim House

Bloomfield, Connecticut

Library of Congress Control Number: 2022909505

ISBN: 979-8-9855621-3-2

First Edition, 2022

Printed & bound by Ingram Content Group

Book design by Rennie McQuilkin

Front cover photograph by Jean Beaufort

Author photograph by Joanna Jacobus

Antrim House
860.519.1804
AntrimHouseBooks@gmail.com
www.AntrimHouseBooks.com
400 Seabury Dr., #5196, Bloomfield, CT 06002

for Joanna

ACKNOWLEDGMENTS

I wish to thank friends who read some of the early versions of poems in this book: Patricia Terry, whose enthusiasm came at a perfect moment; Gwen Gunn, who spotted errors we all missed; Richard Geller, whose shrewd analysis clarified some lines; Eileen Fischer, who was brave enough to tell me what she did not like, and helped me avoid being sloppy; Matthew Proser, whose poems in *Secular Music* inspired me, and whose critique saved me some embarrassment; and Karen Henry, whose book of poems, *All Will Fall Away*, stimulated me to begin this collection. Most of all, of course, was the constant support and love of Joanna through all the years of listening to my poems and asking for more.

TABLE OF CONTENTS

IV. On the Yangtze

V. Hopper's Nighthawks

Memories warm you up from the inside. But they also tear you apart.

–Haruki Murakami

WILDCAT ON THE SHORELINE

I. A SENSE OF TOUCH

A Sense of Touch

There are nights
lying awake on my side
feeling fingers touch my back
that I think it must be the spirit
of my child.
            I check the clock
to see it is the hour and minute
when she died holding her brother's
hand.
            And when I have such
a nighttime visitation again I don't
need the clock to know
what time it is.
I sense the touch
of fingers so real,
so palpable that
it must be a reassurance,
a way of telling me she
has not forgotten, just as I
have not forgotten.

Reincarnate

It surprised me when my Catholic cousin
said that she had worked out the problem
of life after death by determining that it
would be a satisfying solution to be reborn
in another form of life. She did not mention
genera, or even species. I had the feeling that
she was happy with the thought that whatever
was her future fate, it would have eyes, and
possibly ears with which to enjoy the world
that she had temporarily left behind. She did
not mention fangs or poison glands or razor
teeth, although all of those gifts were on my
mind when I thought it over. For me, being
an orchid would suffice. Or maybe a rose.

Late Night Thoughts

Dinner over, drinks in the other room,
I sat it out alone. Talk steady, they went on
but I was too sober, too stretched that night
so I sat there with a book on my lap and
the woman with beautiful breasts came
in as if checking up.
                         The party was far
from done. I knew that. I wasn't playing hard
to get, or playing some social game like
the intellectual who had years before
amused me by leaving us all because he
was bored.
                    I was not bored. I was tired
and needed some silence. But she came
in and sat on the arm of the chair.
"What happens after this, do you think?"
She asked me.
                    "What happens?"
"Where do we go after this?" the look
on her face told me she meant not
after this lovely dinner, not after the
group decided to go. "Is there anything
after this?" she said, and I knew she
was serious. "Where do we go?"
                                        She
really wanted an answer.
"I expect to go," I said, "back to
wherever I was when Hannibal crossed
the Alps." I didn't mention his African
elephants or how long ago that was. But

I did mean it.
    She thought for a while, a little
tipsy, I knew, but still lovely, and touching
my forehead, rose and as she joined the others
I heard her call for another white wine.

Dreams

Sometimes they are so real
and the places so exotic

Sometimes people see me
and I melt like frost in the wind

Sometimes I am totally lost
and the map of return is a butterfly

Sometimes I am in a strange university
and the lectures are dripping candle wax

Sometimes I am standing on a corner
and the stones give way beneath me

Sometimes I hear my voice imploring
and the faces before me blur in laughter

Sometimes I am making love with a woman
and tenderness takes charge of my soul

Sometimes I am running through streets
and the darkness makes me invisible

Sometimes the scene is innocuous
and I wonder who I am

Sometimes I realize I am dreaming
and the person who is me is not me

Sometimes my dreams reveal the truth
and I wander off in silence and awe

A Concert Grand

It is holding, she said. Stable in tune,
this old sleeping giant,
                         Eileen's
Steinway. Purchased second hand
in 1918, the joy of her youth.

In 1970 Florida, considered
a useless relic, even Sharon
wrote it off.
                But today
It sounds like a throaty colossus.
So huge, so black, so deep, so fine.

Haydn's *Adagio in F* seems wedded to
its case, frame, and harp.
                         Every note a
discovery, music sounding from its
soul and made real—as the poet Ezra
said, *news that stays news.*

My Sister

The years
between us, greater than the miles,
made our lives different, and both
Catholic, we each felt guilt that we
could not share.
                            She
married when I was six and disappointed
her mother. She must have felt the power
of guilt only mothers can impose. She
suffered divorce, of course, and ungrateful
children looming in the future,
but somehow she overcame pains that
might have stopped most.
                                        Too young
to help her, too unworldly, too self- involved,
too far away in space and time,
I feel guilt for not being there
when things were bad.
                                    I could
have helped when she took refuge in the
Church, nursing in a saints' home
where elderly priests repented and nuns
thought about the sins of the past and the
suffering of their patients.
                                        When a lightning
hemorrhage struck our Doris she rested in
the care of the church.
Three priests said
her funeral mass. A room received
her open coffin. The liturgical

rose-colored candlelight,
the Byzantine incense,
and soft murmurs of prayer
were her reward.

Four Roses

When my email subject
line is one word,
one name:
Bill
Jim
Mike
Andy
Linda
Norman
I know instantly
another friend failed
to live to be a hundred.

Yet, what's this about
centenarians having an uptick
in the next few decades?

My diet is Mediterranean
and my exercise designed
for extenuation.
        My mind is
constantly in thrall of word
games like poems, twisters,
cryptograms, and sympathy
letters that always say the
same thing differently.
           No
more smoking, but yes the
odd Zinfandel/Shiraz blend,
and, yes, Red Label before
dinner, all for cardiac insurance.

Nevertheless
my name on your email subject
line will be very short.

Luck is what my medicine man
tells me makes the difference.
My aunt Pat cursed her luck
when she was 102. "Why
doesn't he take me?" she
asked her daughter who
smuggled in a slug of Four
Roses each evening at bed
time.

Bourbon, not the Mediterranean
diet, sustained her. Eventually,
she died of complications,
which is to say, of being 104.

The notice arrived in the mail
because she was an old-fashioned girl.

Feathers

Putting a sweater away
in the lowest drawer at
the start of spring,
I looked forward to sultry days.

Then my head filled with feathers.

In extreme slow-
motion, I aimed my body upward,
but leaned like that tower in Italy
and fell.
          I observed it all,
fearing fatality, the end
not just of winter, but
of all winters.
My body's failures
are now commonplace:
                    The terror
comes when my brain deceives my mind.

Vespers

It was a boat trip,
really nothing more.
A little tour on a small
boat up and down the
Connecticut River
looking for eagles
poised above the icy floe.

Five quiet young men
cloistered with one another
as we tourists binoculared
ourselves from right to left,
glimpsing hooded raptors
far above, Godlike,
meditating, aware
but indifferent.

Now on land, we stayed
listening to Vespers.
The young postulants
transformed the evening into a
revelation of the holiness of
earth, water, and sky through
the human voice, itself
another form of nature's beauty.

Consciousness Is a Talon

Said to be the hard problem,
consciousness evolved early,
only thousands of millennia
after the eye.
Like the eye,
it aims to examine,
respond, imagine,
discover,
and destroy.
       Like
sharp teeth, and ravaging
claws, it can wound
and savage its prey.
          But, then,
considering the stars,
it can conceive
the holy, and inspire.

II. WILDCAT ON THE SHORELINE

Wildcat on the Shoreline

I saw the wildcat one night
busy at a kill. It hovered over its meal
and stared into the lights of my car. I waited,
but like all the beasts I see, it did not fear me.
Indeed it knew I feared it more.
But this night I waited, speaking softly as if
it were a pet. It made not a sound until it
rose from its meal and with an unreal cough
leaped up the grassy mound and over the lichened
stone fence behind our house and dissolved into
the darkness.
            Weeks later it was back
preying on our neighbors' chickens
across the street. When challenged,
the wildcat lowered itself
to the grass and refused to stir.
My neighbor and her child
shouted, threatened, waved their arms,
but the wildcat knew there were
more chickens waiting behind
the wire.
            The black bear sighted two houses
away was almost friendly by comparison.
Almost cuddly as it wobbled off toward
the streams and through the trees
up and away past the granite ridge.

Full Moon in Winter

At two in the morning the moon
pauses overhead. I stand by the
window after climbing out of bed.

What always shocks me is the
illusion of snow on the grass below,
the expanse of lawn in a pewter glow.

This is winter and the night should be
dark and thoughtful, filled with dreams,
but the moon's dominance fills me

with admiration. It is a kind of victory
over sleep, over winter, over death,
if only for an evening's few hours. The

moon etches the roof's crossbeam
on the grass – that much is dark. The
shadow of the old spruce leans a stark

impossible angle toward the road. What
thrills me is how absolute the shadows
are, how distinct each branch, each line

of the barren trees. And the color
wavers between a ghostly green and
a reassuring blue, all moon-lit but

definite. This, I realize, is the time for
rituals and celebrations in the open
marches of the woods, when the moon

pulls not only on the oceans, but on
our pulsing blood, calling us to
illuminate the darkness in our soul.

Bluebirds Sipping Water in Our Birdbath

Ten days with no rain, I
filled the wobbly bird bath
bleached in the morning sun.
For no good reason, I tampered
with nature, I thought. But
who doesn't want to nudge
spring or move the world
along a bit?
    What was that
about the butterfly's wings
in the Andes and a pile-up
on the 5 in Los Angeles?
      So,
aware I was stepping into
deep waters I leveled
the birdbath slightly,
avoiding the inch-and-a-half high
daffodils on my right
and the apparent hibiscus
on my left as I stepped away.
      Inside,
over the sink washing my hands,
I looked out on
the arrival of two chubby
Bluebirds, a nesting pair.
So rare, carefully sipping
in unison.
    A gift to me this
spring, their flight so much more
powerful than the legendary butterfly
and likely to cause so much more

excitement in Halifax or Olympia
that I felt I had begun an unending
cycle of wonderful things.
                              Two
Bluebirds sipping water in our birdbath.

White Tails

The deer treat our place like a grocery,
eating any flower we think is lovely
and inspiring. When I see four or five
breakfasting, I wander out carelessly
so as not to spook them, and they
pause stolid and still, trying to
imagine what I am doing there on
two legs instead of four. They
don't see feathers, maybe not
even the color of my pajamas.

Getting the Mail

I thought, as I approached my
wobbly letter box, of Coleridge,
who said, "The truly great
have all one age," like a
piece of mail from beyond,
a message that makes me
think the truly dead
are also all one age, and I
see myself dedicated to
a future shared not with
the great, but with the rest.

Then, above me, in the
frozen air below the clouds
a turkey buzzard sailed as
they all do, effortlessly,
her call harsh, almost cruel
and barking, unlike any
other raptor I ever heard.

Bird omens are common
but this buzzard screamed,
"Ruschs!" like a mastiff.

I watched, stopped
and watched. She
made me think of Hopkins,
and ask if this bird was
my morning's minion,
showing me nature's layering of

road, river, air, and sky
including a protest – "Ruschs!"
as signifying a drama
whose last act is drawing near.

Snap Dragon

Late in the spring evening
we heard the soft feathery "hoo"
announcing a partnership.

I yearned to see its form
in the dark, but no luck –
it remained inchoate.

A direct observation
like my own expression
of wordless satisfaction.

Just a message of presence
meaning *I am here*
meaning *I too participate.*

But the wee mouse
climbing the brick chimney
to the attic was unaware that

the peanut butter snap dragon
awaited him, his unhappy
journey taking him back

to nature. In the morning
I stretched him on the granite
block near the hickory sapling,

the whiteness of his soft
underbelly a badge the owl
might recognize as reward

for attending to us at night
and for understanding
that we are partners of a kind.

Warm Mist Cushions

Warm mist cushions
the sky, sits on the snow.
I cannot take my walk,
cannot risk another fall
so I wait until the ash stands forth
from the barren slopes.

The spruce has made its entrance
and what looks like a
young chestnut
waves its slender arms.

Some would say that woods
are talking to me,
but I hear only the
slurp of dying icicles
in an unannounced mid-February
heatstroke.
   Not a wave, just a momentary
interruption of ice and windchill.
This shallow landscape yields
to the air, drinks the brew
of almost spring.

We who are quarantined applaud
the slightest offer of relief –
an acknowledgment of nature.

Our Bridge Is Down

I can see it from here and they say
we cannot cross over it until spring
when the red oaks and our aging
maple will make it invisible again.

Yesterday four does circled the house
and left a pattern of purposeful tracks
in the snow, leaping our fence and over
the road, on their way to the water.

Our bridge is no inconvenience for them,
the way it restricts us from heading east
and up Breakneck Hill Road. We counted
on it to link us to our friends and our future.

It was always too narrow. We sometimes
cursed the rails scouring the passenger
side of our car. But we also marveled
at the optimism of fishermen leaning

over its south side, where the deeper water
sometimes encouraged brook trout to bite.
There may have been a season to fish the stream,
but we never kept track. And we never saw fish.

In the February sunshine my walk takes me
to its edge. Earth mover and crane arch nearby
and I meditate on bridges, the ones that brought
my father home, the empty one we crossed

one blizzarding Christmas Eve going to Brooklyn.
Such thoughts bring me back to childhood,
itself a bridge one crosses only once,
and, like ours, it heads only westward.

The Red and the Black

Last year I was proud of the
two red-tail hawks who suddenly
appeared on the lawn's verge, large
as our neighbor's chickens. But angry
looking, even noble in a killer's fashion.

Later one rose with a flattened squirrel
into the old oak rising on the granite
ridge. A perfect dinner for one, but
crows attacked from high and low,
demanding a raven's fee of carrion
and got it.
                I'm certain not to be alone
wherever I walk. I am only one of the animals
who have survived civilization near
our lake.
                Why, once walking on the woody
path to see the faithful swans sail white against
the lily pads, we came upon a pair of huge
entwined Black Racers copulating in the grass.
Their tails made a distinct and unmistakable
Rattling.
                We were too near. They were
six feet long and, without separating,
threatened us as mightily
as they could. We backed up slowly,
marveling at their anger and their joy.
They were right to think we're interlopers
and we have been warned.

Feer Fir Féar

High in our ancient oaks
the familiar cry told me
our Red-Shouldered hawk
longed for food. I
found it there on a limb,
its beak working itself
into a frenzy. *Feer! Feer!*
again and again, high-
pitched, anxious, intense,
its speckled breast telling
me he was young, but he
was formidable, a cold
killer, now searching for
prey among the innocent.
As he strained to announce
himself, a Cardinal dove
into the security of a
fir tree.
      Fir from *vir*
in Latin is like a man
protecting prey
from the killer's gaze.
Féar is Irish for grass,
and *féar ocrach*, hungry grass,
threatens all innocents.
Feer! Feer! should chill me,
make me fear the hungry grass.
But, transfixed, I chose
the ferocity of life.

Windows

Why do I always think
of Shakespeare when our rough
maple turns bright bisque
overnight?
           In myself I behold
fall's changes through the window,
where I check the portent
of the sky and the mirroring of the grass.
My maple goes first, then the hickory,
and the beech.
            Acorns explode in
our driveway like artillery
signaling winter's campaign,
but the oaks hold
as they do in spring.
            I look
through the bright new woods
in the morning, then savor
the darkness in the evening.
This cycle will continue and
change. I rally, hoping it will continue
knowing that one day it will not.

III. CHILDHOOD

Childhood

The most important thing about it is
that it seemed to take forever. The years
did not move the way they do today.

Instead, they staggered from infancy
to subtlety. My vague memory begins
with a view through the slats of my playpen.

Its webbing sagged as I jumped, holding the
rail, grinning with the cunning of the man
who leapt into the bay from San Quentin.

My nonagenarian Aunt Mary, demented
and savage, appearing like an angel,
leaned far over, pulling my golden hair

whenever she found me protesting my
incarceration. Always hopeful, I rollicked
toward her, too unworldly to know she

was going to tease and garble at me while
she grabbed handfuls and sang incomprehensible
Irish tunes as if my hair were strings in

Boann's sleepy harp in the ancient Irish days.
Where were people who could have held her
back? Why was I her yelling infant toy?

Before language helped me understand
her painful form of family affection,
I took her long white stringy hair

into my own hands, and with a full body
fall, pulled her ancient bones into my prison,
ending for all time her ravages. And her love.

Byron in the Bookcase

My anger, or maybe disappointment,
moved me to the bookcase
in our new house on Sanford Street,
where I had a bedroom of my own.

With my father deep in the kitchen
out of sight, I burrowed into
one of the lower shelves – I was nine –
and pulled one book out after another
until a soft red volume opened on the
flat of my palm.
                    And I read, "Maid
Of Athens, ere we part, give oh give
me back my heart," and I felt a
pain, a deep yearning.
                            In my agony
I declared I was running away
and left the house in a swagger.
I didn't know romanticism had taken
me, but I knew I had to leave
and make my life over.
                            My wise
father looked out the door and watched
me go. Then he went back into the kitchen.

He knew I could not cross the busy streets,
and when I returned he placed the lemonade
and the sandwich before me without a word.

Windmill

There is that picture of me in
the Windmill H.S. yearbook,
looking to the right, my
hair coiffed high above
my bright and eager eyes.

My friends wrote many
pleasant and imaginative
things in fluid ink around
my face, telling me how we
would all have wonderful lives.

And I can't help but wonder
who I was then, seventy years
later. Eager, yes, friendly, yes,
and happy to move on.
But also insecure and anxious.

What prompts my thoughts
is the question of how much
I am still the same person, or
if time has left me only a
shadow of that boy's soul
and a wisp of his heart.

Webster Place

Childhood was a place,
a house, a time, a street.
Remembered,
it was the smell and touch
of Ginkgo trees, irregular
bluestone slabs on sidewalks
rising and falling with the
season, the arch of the
gutter filled with leaves,
stones, muddy water,
the old fashioned cars
on both sides of the street,
bulging fenders, threatening
chrome gouging us after
every missed toss of the ball,
every race to be the first,
the best, the last, the one.

Evenings on the porch.
Long sessions in rocking chairs.
Neighbors passing silent, curious,
we poised above, looking down,
sometimes acknowledging with a
wave, a smile, a hallo.
              We read
with a jar full of lightning bugs
while Japanese beetles savaged our
Hydrangea. Neighbor radios
echoed a crackling chorus.
Only the cicadas sang with

more enthusiasm.

Childhood was a summer's day
and a long hot humid evening.

Grandpa

What did I call you? I think of you now,
knowing you must have called me by name. But
what name? You died too young, and I was too
unaware at four to think of formal
names. At that age I abbreviated everything.
My dad was Nern and I was Tuck, but
what were you, grandpa? Was it Pa? Gran?

When we went to the market for chops
you chid me for running my car on the
display and that little thing spoiled my day.
I remember that, but little more.

You rode on your bicycle to a job
I never understood. It took you away
and brought you back, until the day
your heart failed.
                    You
now exist in a single photograph,
holding me when I was weeks old. Now older
than you by decades, I do not look like
you. I doubt I think as you thought, believe
what you believed, experience life as
you did, or labor as you labored.
                                    For
all our differences, and for all the
damage done to memory, I loved you
in the way only a four-year-old can love
in response to tenderness, sweetness,
attention, and a love I could not name.

Neighborhood

Crowded near our neighbors,
with whom we rarely spoke,
on a street across from grander homes,
our house fronted a narrow world.

Choked with old autos, the road
was built for horse and carriage
with no driveways, no way out,
and for most of us, no place to go.

At sunset the lamplighter's match
made antique gaslights glimmer.
Once we heard an hysterical woman
crying to no one in the half-dark.

Pride kept us firm behind the blinds,
suspicion sharpened the shadows
of people moving through the evening
mist, and fear locked us in at night.

Leaves

The memory of burning leaves,
the crisping of Oaks and Maples,
of majestic Chestnuts and Elms,
the Sycamore, the Beech, all
gathered as if for a symposium
of autumn, bring an aroma
back to imagination and with it
my childhood, which itself lives
only in memory, and which like
those leaves was consumed,
not by fire but by time.

Since Then . . .

I.

"Bless me, father, for I have sinned. . ."
And there were sins I'd not yet learned,
but simply imagined; and those imaginings
were sins I'd not have confessed until
after, when it was far too late
to go back and wring the soutane in
repentance or kneel on damp stones,
stiff from fear of forgetting the one
thing of highest importance: that
sin which crawled and burrowed itself
deep into the shadowy regions
of memory, where fear itself lurked
like a spider waiting to strike.

II.

"Bless me, father, for I have sinned . . ."
And the sin would wrench my hands
into prayer until words came slowly,
beggarly into my mouth, and dry
lips articulated sound so far
from my soul that the spider would twitch
and the lordly act of confession
become greater temptation to sin.

III.

"And how many times, my son?"
the voice would say, and I would
rest while numbers floated quickly
to mind, while culpability
took a calm, mathematical
form, while sin compounded sin
harmlessly like Euclid's
sinless abstractions. New
transgressions blossomed, each
with its separate arithmetic,
and each its separate pause
for memory to wash itself clean.

IV.

And alone in the darkness, my mind
giving in to the wood and the stone
and the incantatory voice behind
the grill, I'd take refuge in
the line of women waiting on hard
brown benches for my place, their
kerchiefs drawn tightly over
their heads, their shoes large and
masculine as their legs crossed.
They would be there when the curtain
fell back, and the air would caress
me like a sea-breeze, and the virgin
would stand, a blue-and-white gift
from the darkness, and the prayers
would rattle on my tongue like marbles
spilling on tile.

Church Matters

Until scandals revealed perversion hid
behind the veil of sanctification,

we went to Our Lady Help of Christians,
a pile of whitened stone, colored glass,

and large brown doors with huge brass
handles I never touched. Not yet a man,

I struggled through the ritual. Now I
understand that sometimes we should kneel

and sometimes stand. But then all I could feel
was confusion and uncertainty about

how to behave. I soon began to doubt
the ways of priest and nun, the dark terror

of the soutane and coarse dismissal. When
hoping for instruction, I was accosted by a

dark sodality in an anteroom of
suspicion, with a priest, his retinue

of boys, his choir of thugs whose
song was humiliation and control.

I knew without being told that it was
not the time to kneel but the time to stand.

IV. ON THE YANGTZE

On the Yangtze

Was it two or three
in the morning,
steaming toward
Chungking in a
fog that could
have blanketed
the world.
        I sat
on my cot
looking out
and seeing
nothing, only
hearing nearby
boats in the
turbid waters,
thinking *I may
not live through
this, may not
get back to land
or see the ones
I love and do I
have any idea
what the meaning
of my life is?*

Flamenco

In Seville the dancers
stamp their heels,
square their arms
above their head
and thrill us with
their arrogance, their
percussive violence
drilling the floor
into submission.

Then Amaya waves
her castanets, first
softly, then in that
rhythm signifying
passion in the Spanish
heat, signifying sex
and superiority, her
toes fleeting with
such speed as to
bate our breath,
and we hold our
selves suspended
in time as the guitars
shear the dance
while she suggests
what Lorca once
called *Duende*.

The Great Wall of China

Raincoat-hooded women
swept the slope and
the snowy street below.

Before us, the winding
road upward, and the vast
landscape to the west.

But here a Chinese child grasped
my hand and cried with joy
as her mother took our picture.

For a few moments we were
tourists all, discovering
each other, not just a wall.

History in the Streets

People were in the streets with hundreds
daring to challenge the guards. They were
staring into uncertainty, picturing themselves
later as actors in history.
                              Much of the talk
today is about making history, but no one
really knows what that means. In reality
history is always forgotten, a virtual talisman
that is kissed, blessed, praised, and ignored.

What brutal cop has killed another black man
on the side of the road, in the gutter,
in the street by the dime store while a girl
looks at the image on her smart phone
registering it all. For history?
                              Is it history
because it happens now, or is it history
because it happened yesterday, last week,
last season, or 1941 with Emmet Till
or 2021 with George Floyd?
                              The dead
pile up historically, each one another instance
of our disgrace celebrated with flowers, candles,
images and signs all demanding memory,
writing in the streets like dates incised on stelae.
Orators eulogize these moments as indelible marks
on the tablet of time.

But the flowers wilt, the candles shutter,
the images fade. What remains are names and dates,
a history of darkness.

The News

By God, is there no relief!
Centuries ago in the mountains
near Lake Shang a wise merchant,
seeking piety and consolation,
said, "The sky is high
and the government is in Peking."

Today the wise merchants
of China rule the Eastern world.
The government is now in Beijing
but no matter how high the sky
it touches the bureaucrat in Omaha,
the sailor in New London, the bigot
in Dallas, the senator in Maine,
and the soldier in his foxhole
everywhere.

American Romance

The hero in a perfect grey uniform
confronted Grant, clothes spotted
with the clay of Gettysburg.
Lee sat high on his horse. Grant
chewed on a cheroot in deshabille.

Birth of a Nation and *Gone with the Wind*
made citizens long for the romantic South.
People applauded when statues loomed
in imitation of victory and success.
Lee on horseback, Jefferson Davis in the
capitol, anonymous rebels in small towns
like Granbury, Texas. They came down
with cries of cancelling history.

But where were the statues of Benedict
Arnold and Major Andre?
They were history too.

And to honor history we need
statues of the Pequot and Lenape.
We need statues of slave children
coming in from the fields
after the day's toil.
General Lee was history
for four years. Slaves in Virginia
were history for four centuries.
Where are their statues?

The Pyramids

Standing before the pyramids,
I could only think of my father
who marveled at the ingenuity
of ages past. He never got to see
them, or roam through the streets
of Cairo. He did not sail up the Nile
to Abu Simbel with those gigantic
faces staring into the future,
scorning us all for all time,

But he, unscorned and untaught,
regarded the ancients with awe,
as he should – as I did when
looking into the dark entrance of Giza,
hesitating there next to the gigantic
blocks of stone larger than some of the
cars I had owned.

Like him, all I could think
was *How could they have done this?*
What great faith, what great magic,
what great willingness pushed them on
to make it to the top?

And how did all this become a
tourist attraction vested with mystery, yes,
but an attraction with men reduced to selling
postcards and hawking camels? Yes, I was
put upon a silent beast and raised to a height
that made me fear for my life, then sent

forward with others, all fearful that
the beast would walk out upon the desert
and not return, would leave us to crisp
in the sun and become timeless.

Afghans and Watermelons

Before the wars,
somewhere outside Lashkar Gah
Joel Baldwin shot the photo
of two men lounging on the ground
before a white-plastered home
treated with delicate decorations
in faded sapphire that might
identify a face or a place.
Two large triangles beside
an open door. Dots connecting
them like a telegraph. In another
country these might symbolize
Christmas trees. Here they can
only imply a prayer.

The old man
studies his hand on his upright knee;
the younger looks at Joel,
neither interested nor apprehensive.
These men are at peace, lackadaisical
merchants with a stack of twenty-nine
watermelons next to them.

Before them on a large round tray
are piles of green grapes. It may be
hot, but each turbaned man wears
blousy trousers, a white shirt, and
typical vests. Nothing stirs.

Joel recalled it being warm and lush.
A good day
for watermelons in Lashkar Gah.

V. HOPPER'S NIGHTHAWKS

Hopper's Nighthawks

We like it because it demands
a story, has all the elements
of a mystery. It's late at night
with a set of emotions built in:
disappointment, something we
know about in our bones;
apprehension in the sharp-
nosed man who looks ready
for another cup of coffee;
defeat, in the back of the
figure who is said to be
Hopper himself.

His wife modeled for the woman
who examines a matchbook or
a small folder of cash.
Is she paying the bill or thinking
about a career in art?

The late night diner is pure Noir.
We suspect that John Garfield and
Ann Sheridan just left. Or is it where
Burt Lancaster picked up a cup of
java before holing up, waiting
for the killers?

The empty road,
the stark colors, the triangulation of
yellow and green, red and brown,
all intensify the brilliance of

the finger-pointing yellow walls
and the sense that something
has happened.

A Walk on the Canal with Olga Rudge

We began with drinks
and talked of Venetian light
on the baked walls of
Dorsaduro. Olga's daughter
was in town for a talk, so
she would see her later.
Now, we were poised on the
balcony with Jim, who had
invited us for a literary moment.
Olga was stately, dressed in
a brown Houndstooth suit,
a small woolen hat on gray hair,
dainty, in a way, but despite her
90 years, strong, direct, intense.

When the sun began to fade
I offered to walk her home
and took her hand. We trailed
the Rio Fornace off the Grand
Canal all the way to Calle Quirini.
Once there, she graciously
asked me in to see the home she
and Ezra shared for so many years.

It was tiny, dark at first, with a foot-high
board at the door to keep swells out.
Olga talked of him, still fresh in her mind,
and showed me the rickety wooden box
he put together for a desk. Her father gave
her this house in the 1920s. It contained

her still. Upstairs in the bedroom the
lamp shone on a small framed photograph
of her and Ezra standing on a park-like path.
She was pictured in her Houndstooth suit.
It was before the war. They were at peace.

Defoe's Journal

In the midst of a plague
of our own, I turned to
you for insight.
Camus looked into your Journal
too, but his take was
metaphorical, a peek into
politics.

Of course my view
was also political and maybe
even rhymed with Camus,
but we were living with the
threat of death, in the range
of danger, given our age
and medical conditions.
So I was focused on what you
saw in St. Giles in the Fields,
Cripplegate, Hounds-Ditch,
Epping and Southwark.

Our numbers grew prodigiously,
like yours, in Washington, New York,
Texas, North Dakota, and
California. Just as you indicated,
it was contagious, borne in air,
and the rich went away from the
city and bunked in cabins
while the poor were told to stay inside.

You said shuttering the houses
was not a solution. People crept out

at night, watchmen were bribed,
some simply scoffed and held court
in taverns, opening the windows
to mock and jeer at the lamentations
of those whose dead were carted by.

We refrigerated our dead in the first
year, but scoffers cycled wildly.
New Orleans marched its bands
and carnivalled its skeleton crews,
while celebrations of spring on
Southern beaches raised the stakes.

You said some Londoners felt
a rage to infect others. Our people
infected others casually, in Rose
Gardens, Rallies, and Insurrection.
You mentioned astrologers and
masks – the former died, the masks
worked. Our astrologers were on TV,
masking the truth, denying reality,
zealously producing a second
and third wave of deaths.

You would
have known the truth were you here.
You could have told us how the poor
were pressed together and always at
risk, dying in pain or grieving alone.
You knew the clergy would talk about
God's judgment and man's sinfulness,
while demanding attendance
in superstore mega-churches. You

knew that when it was all over
people would have learned little
from the Plague, despite promises
to change.
            You would
feel at home here.

Sitting for David Brown

Walking about the Stupa,
tossing ashes in the air
and holding hands
through the prayer.

The daffodils
punctuated every murmur,
every moment of joy,
sharing something sacred.

A Tibetan moment
with friends in the sunshine
of spring, with reverence for
continuation, not change. Where
was the spirit in us? Where
could we find the interior of our soul?

 II

He sat us down in the cold
studio, a huge canvas before him,
smoking without stop,
dipping his brush in some blend
of solvent and oil, stopping to talk
about the process, what looked wrong.

We dared not move, thinking
of where we had been days before,
how we had studied the air
as if it held content for the impression

he wanted for his brush,
the danger of looking like those
famous farmers in Chicago,
rake in one hand and gloom
in the other.

What did he see as he tinted our
skin, as he drafted my jacket,
which he feared he would never
get right? And didn't.

So many days talking while he
brushed us on the canvas.
Eventually we had to leave
for Texas. He was not
satisfied then, but somehow it all
came together after we left,
after we abandoned our places
in the canvas chairs and left
him with the echo of our spirit.
Had we been sitters or sutras?

When we were not there to be seen,
David got it right. He saw
what was unseen because we
no longer sat in the way of his seeing.

Later we did a victory lap
about the Stupa,
its yellow and white surfaces gleaming
like flowers in a flag from another country.

Reading Trollope

Yes, he told the truth about himself
and made his readers wonder why
they tolerated all his money-making
and his almost cynical approach to the
art of literature.

And, yes, every tale
is timed to the second, timed to the exact
word, trimming thoughts and wistfulness,
ambition, anxiety, delusion and passion
all to the same fit, as if into a purse
or a lady's reticule.

His themes are much
the same. Can there be that many fathers
who tolerate wastrels and dominate their
daughters? Can there be that many young
women who manage matrimonial prospects
with the precision of accountants? Can there
be that many young men chivying for position
in politics, or lusting for Bishopricks?

All seems contrived, yet all so obviously true
that one sees the world through his eyes
and admits his basic views are real.
When love blinds lovers, all seems to end well,
but when it is occult, uncertain, unflowering,
it is all the more true to our understanding. Sex
is his dark matter permitting the young to wait
years for marriage. He is the Attenborough
of mating rituals. His biology interprets nothing

less than money and its many miraculous oughts,
following simple numbers, making life
possible. He tells the truth about love and
the truth about money. And he does it again,
and again, and again. The very faith he
practiced is there in his books of revelation.

Thinking About Love

It is one thing to examine the color of hawthorns
white or pink, aggressive or calm, as spring unfurls.

And it is a great comfort to sit by the ocean sands
startled by late afternoon reflections on the surge.

Such things are miracles of reality, like the hibiscus
that pushes itself up through the loam in April.

Those things are palpable and ripe for meditation
but where are desire and anticipation, love and hate?

At times I feel ravaged by desire, hounded by anticipation,
and mellowed by reflections on the hopefulness of love.

When I think of love it is not love, but those I have loved
that come to mind – that are thought of, remembered.

I can write about love, write about desire, and reflect
on what is written. Love itself resists my thoughts.

What is written is not love, but words, and I can think
of words just as I can think of laurels in the forest.

I want to think about love but cannot hope to see it
in the world of color and substance surrounding me.

Yet its reality yields every day to a world of feeling.
Feeling, not thinking, is my means of apprehension.

Did I know this as a child? Love's demands dominate
childhood, only to blossom much later, not as an idea

but as a touch – not as a thought, but as a feeling,
an apprehension surpassing thought.

Charles Olson in Mansfield

In the grass on
Wormwood Hill Road, he
stood to his full height,
six-foot seven, and declaimed,
"Man's Field!" finding great significance
in his arrival.

He found significance
in every motion, every
moment, every utterance.

He looked down on me and asked, "What
do you teach?" I told him, "Milton,"
and that was the only moment
I saw him hesitate, almost remain silent,
until he said, "That's a real subject."

So also was Charles Olson a real subject in
Connecticut, dressing down his former students
for having no work to show, pursuing
a female seminarian who was six feet tall:
"I didn't mean you," he said, following her
down the hall after chasing out the overflow
students in his class. And she returned, a
chosen one.

The Maximus Poem was
unending, like the overflow of Vesuvius,
pouring forth a voice that commanded
life itself.

As he lay in the hospital in Windham,
his doctor said his cancer had begun in the
Maxilla bone. Charles Olson heard
and cried, "The Maximus Bone!"

I felt I hardly
knew him before he was gone from Man's Field.

Messes

I live with messes,
with incompleteness.
Books next to my feet,
calling me back
to what I left unfinished.

Books on the desk.
I just counted them, thirteen
on the left, thin
shiny books of poems
by people I know,
or should know.

But in hard-cover magnificence
on the right, lie Eliot, Cummings,
Stevens, Hall, Bishop, Glück,
all in disarray.

Like the Egyptian
god Anubis, they await my
ka and *ba*, an eternal judgment
asking if I have served,
if my messes resulted from
seeking beauty in disorder,
in randomness,
in the willingness
to let one's soul meander

resisting a call to
settle for perfection.

Walking Poems

We all feel regret for what the man
from Porlock did to Kubla Khan.
Coleridge lost the rest of his poem
by engaging with the business world.

But the marvelous thing for me
is that he composed his poems
walking, or maybe pausing near
the Wye to watch a twig or leaf
wander down river in that ecstasy
that moves us on a summer day
when all is done, all is awaiting
us in anticipation of a return
to someone we love.

His special friends did much the same,
making poetic music as they walked,
tuning themselves to their saunter,
a rhythm of genius.

The Layered Look

I stood like a tweeded laird
on the far side of a stone
wall, poised as if in a novel
by Sir Walter Scott,
or maybe serving a spot of haggis,
which I once had prepared
for me at Storrs, when I
was young and literature served as
my guide to living well.

This morning I went into the
frozen air tweeded and layered
like the old man I am, a liberal
conservative, friend of Milton,
but in conversation with Amiri
Baraka, who, when we talked
was a model of cordiality.

My guide to living well and fully
is still literature.

ABOUT THE AUTHOR

Lee A. Jacobus, Professor of English Emeritus at the University of Connecticut, Storrs, taught poetry, Milton, Shakespeare, and modern Anglo-Irish literature. His poems have appeared in *The Carolina Quarterly*, *The Literary Review*, *Michigan Quarterly*, *Other Voices* (Chicago), and elsewhere. Among his books are *Crown Island, Volcanic Jesus, A World of Ideas, The Humanities Through the Arts, The Bedford Introduction to Drama, Shakespeare: The Dialectic of Certainty,* and others. He lives on the Connecticut Shoreline with Joanna Jacobus, who taught dance and choreography at the University of Connecticut and Eastern Connecticut University.

This book is set in Garamond Premier Pro, which had its genesis in 1988 when type-designer Robert Slimbach visited the Plantin-Moretus Museum in Antwerp, Belgium, to study its collection of Claude Garamond's metal punches and typefaces. During the fifteen hundreds, Garamond – a Parisian punch-cutter – produced a refined array of book types that combined an unprecedented degree of balance and elegance, for centuries standing as the pinnacle of beauty and practicality in type-founding. Slimbach has created a new interpretation based on Garamond's designs and on compatible italics cut by Robert Granjon, Garamond's contemporary.

Copies of this book can be ordered
from all bookstores including Amazon
or directly from Lee A. Jacobus
1 Laconia Dr.
Clinton, CT 06413-8028.
Send $18 per book
plus $4 shipping
by check payable
to Lee A. Jacobus.

•

For more information on the work of Lee Jacobus
visit www.antrimhousebooks.com/authors.html.
The author can be contacted at
leejacobus@aol.com.